See You Tomorrow, Brother

Written by Tommy Watkins

To my brother Brad and the adventures we shared

growing up together.

The perfect fort was built, with sleeping bags rolle

out.

The video game system turned onto the television

But wait! They forgot their favorite candy!

The boys tiptoed up the stairs to the kitchen. So th

parents don't wake up!

The boys find their perfect candy, and they tiptoe

back downstairs.

Eager to play against each other, they start the via

game. Eating candy and competing, they each try

win the match. The match gets loud and intense

"Boys, go to bed!" says their mother, angry and tir

The boys quiet down in fear of their mother comi[ng]

downstairs! The boys put on a movie and eat all t[he]

leftover candy.

Ready to fall asleep to a great movie...

Into the night...

See You Tomorrow, Brother.

The End

Milton Keynes UK
Ingram Content Group UK Ltd.
UKHW051333060924
447877UK00002B/5